CYBER BULLYING

DISCARD

Nick Hunter

Heinemann
LIBRARY

Chicago, Illinois

www.heinemannraintree.com
Visit our website to find out
more information about
Heinemann-Raintree books.

To order:

☎ Phone 888-454-2279

🖥 Visit www.heinemannraintree.com
to browse our catalog and order online.

Edited by Adam Miller, Andrew Farrow, and
Adrian Vigliano
Designed by Clare Webber and Steven Mead
Original illustrations © Capstone Global
Library Ltd.
Picture research by Ruth Blair
Production by Eirian Griffiths
Originated by Capstone Global Library Ltd.
Printed and bound in China by Leo Paper
Products Ltd.

15 14 13 12
10 9 8 7 6 5 4 3

**Library of Congress Cataloging-in-
Publication Data**
Hunter, Nick.
  Cyber bullying / Nick Hunter.
      p. cm.—(Hot topics)
  Includes bibliographical references and
index.
  ISBN 978-1-4329-4869-6 (hc)
  1. Cyberbullying—Juvenile literature. 2.
Bullying—Juvenile literature. 3. Bullying in
schools—Juvenile literature. I. Title.
  HV6773.H88 2012
  302.3—dc22   2010046906

Acknowledgments
The author and publishers are grateful to
the following for permission to reproduce
copyright material: Alamy pp. **5** (© ACE
STOCK LIMITED), **17** (© sandy young), **21**
(© Kuttig – People), **22** (© Angela Hampton
Picture Library), **29** (© Design Pics Inc.),
30 (© Huntstock, Inc.), **32** (© Corbis Super
RF), **47** (© Stock Connection Blue), **49**
(© Bubbles Photolibrary); Corbis pp. **8** (©
Roger Ressmeyer), **14** (© Lucy Nicholson/
Reuters), **24** (© Jack Hollingsworth), **33**
(© Trevor Lush), **36** (© Image Source), **39**
(© Image Source), **40** (© Glowimages),
43 (© Ocean); PA Photos p. **35** (© Tina
Meier/AP); Shutterstock pp. **4** (© Jacek
Chabraszewski), **7** (© photocritical), **9** (©
Monkey Business Images), **10** (© Pixsooz),
13 (© oliveromg), **19** (© Jace Tan), **27** (© PT
Images), **38** (© karamysh).

Cover photograph of shadowy figures
menacing a boy at a computer reproduced
with permission of Alamy (© Mark Phillips).

Every effort has been made to contact
copyright holders of any material reproduced
in this book. Any omissions will be rectified
in subsequent printings if notice is given to
the publisher.

CONTENTS

Some words are printed in bold, **like this**. You can find out what they mean by looking in the glossary.

BULLYING IN YOUR OWN HOME

Kylie Kenney was 15 years old when the bullying started. Two of her classmates had set up a website called "Kill Kylie Incorporated." On the website, they posted nasty and threatening comments about Kylie. Anyone could view the website, including

"I was scared, hurt, and confused. I didn't know why it was happening to me. I had nowhere to turn except to my mom."

Kylie Kenney, victim of cyber bullying

Kylie herself. This was bad enough, but it was not the only way Kylie was being bullied. She also received insulting emails and phone calls. Even worse, the bullies set up **instant messaging (IM)** accounts, using them so they could pretend to be Kylie and send rude messages to her friends. The bullying became so hurtful that Kylie was forced to move to a new school.

The bullying that Kylie experienced—through websites, emails, and IM—is a relatively new type of bullying. In the past, bullies might have **harassed** their victims with teasing or physical violence. But now that most people use computers and cell phones to communicate with friends, bullies can also use these means of communication to hurt people. Bullying that uses **electronic media** like the Internet and cell phones to reach victims is known as cyber bullying.

■ If you are being cyber bullied, you may think you are alone. However, cyber bullying is very common.

No escape

Bullying is a terrible thing to deal with at any time, but cyber bullying can be especially tough. In the past, bullies would target their victims at school, or on the way to and from school. But now that bullies can use websites, email, or text messages, it is much more difficult for victims to escape. Also, as Kylie Kenney found out, bullies can use different names and identities, so victims do not even always know who their attacker is.

Kylie's story may seem very familiar to you. Cyber bullying is not rare. It is estimated that at least 25 percent of teenagers are victims of cyber bullying.

Whether or not you have been affected by cyber bullying, this book will help you to understand different forms of cyber bullying and the actions you can take to stop the bullying. If you have been involved in bullying yourself, this book will give plenty of examples to help you understand the pain your actions have caused. The book will also look at some of the topics linked to cyber bullying, such as protecting your privacy online.

■ Physical bullying is bad enough, but at least the victims are usually safe once they enter their own homes. Victims of cyber bullying cannot get away from their bullies.

WHAT IS CYBER BULLYING?

Bullying is any activity that uses force or threats to **persecute** people and make them feel bad. Cyber bullying is a type of bullying that uses electronic media. People who cyber bully can use email, IM, text messages, and images accessed from a phone or computer. Web pages, **blogs**, chat rooms, and **social networking sites** like Facebook and MySpace can also carry bullying messages and pictures. Cyber bullying is sometimes also called cyber harassment, particularly if it involves adults.

Many of the methods used to cyber bully people are not that different from those used in traditional forms of bullying. In the past, the use of hurtful or threatening messages involved direct, spoken insults. In cyber bullying, harassment usually takes place in the form of electronic messages.

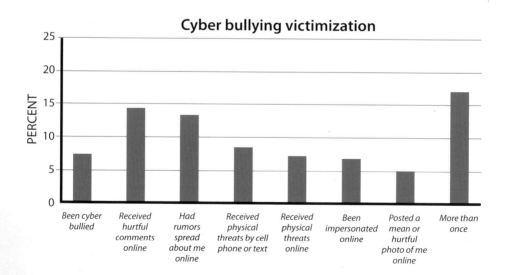

Cyber bullying victimization

There are many different types of cyber bullying. This chart shows the most common types experienced by percentages of students in a southern school district over a 30-day period.

6

A MISUNDERSTANDING?

It is not always easy to decide whether some acts are cyber bullying or not. For example, when does an online argument in a chat room become cyber bullying? People who receive a hurtful message or email may see it as cyber bullying, but the person who sent it may see it as harmless fun.

It can be easy to get involved in this type of bullying. Comments about someone's looks, body shape, or even the sports team they are a fan of can become very hurtful. If you find yourself making jokes or comments online, think about how it will seem to the other person. If the person could misunderstand or not see the joke, or if you are intending to cause offense, then this is cyber bullying.

Spreading information or rumors about someone is another form of bullying. This could either be a false rumor or information that was not intended to be shared. Before the Internet, a rumor might spread around a school. Now it can be spread much more widely, just by forwarding a text message or email.

Impersonation is one type of bullying that is unique to cyber bullying. Online communication makes it much easier for bullies to pretend to be their victims and to send false messages on their behalf.

■ Emails may not always be from whom they seem to be from. Online bullies can pretend to be someone else.

The growth of the Internet …

The term "cyber bullying" did not exist before 2000. Before that time, there was no need for a word to describe this type of bullying. In 2000 only about 40 percent of U.S. adults said that they used the Internet.

Since then, the Internet has become part of almost everyone's life. Think about all the ways that you use computers and the Internet. Of course, you use computers for school and homework. You probably also spend a lot of your leisure time online, communicating with your friends on social networking sites, or using IM. You might even spend time using online multiplayer games.

… and the growth of cyber bullying

Cyber bullying is constantly changing as new electronic media and technologies become popular. As an example, Facebook was only founded in 2004, but it now has hundreds of millions of users. Many of these users are young people. Those who want to cyber bully people often see sites like this as a way to get at their targets.

A lot has changed with computers over a very short time period. The development of the Internet since the 1990s has brought lots of benefits, but it has also brought dangers.

■ Text messaging is a useful technology. But cell phones can be used to send bullying messages.

The increasing use of cell phones

The growth in the use of cell phones has been just as spectacular as the growth of the Internet. In 2004, only 45 percent of U.S. teenagers owned a cell phone. By 2009, more than 8 out of 10 teenagers in the United States owned cell phones. Around the world, there are now more than three cell phones for every computer.

Cameras, Internet access, and other features on **smartphones** mean that these phones are now much more than just a way of keeping in touch. However, the most popular feature of many phones is one of the most simple—text messaging. Around half of U.S. teenagers say that they send more than 50 text messages every day.

As we will explore, developments in technology have been matched by new types of bullying.

TYPES OF CYBER BULLYING

There are many ways that people are cyber bullied. The electronic media that cyber bullies can use—ranging from cell phones to chat rooms and online games—are always changing.

Bullying by phone

Cell phones are great for keeping in touch wherever you are, but they also mean that sometimes you can be contacted by people you do not want to hear from.

Bullying by phone can take lots of different forms. People can be harassed by abusive or threatening text messages or phone calls. This might just be one text message, or it could be hundreds of messages from one person or from a group of people. People may also receive messages containing nasty or offensive pictures. With phone bullying, as with other kinds of cyber bullying, the people sending the bullying message or making the call can easily hide their identities.

Message: 19/10

no 1 likes you

■ It can be very difficult to ignore a bullying text message, but do not reply.

CASE STUDY

Beating the phone bullies

Phoebe was just 10 years old when she was tormented by bullying phone calls and text messages. Every night, Phoebe would receive calls and messages on her phone. "They started phoning me saying that I was in the cow club and that I should phone the loser line and stuff … It was really immature, but really upsetting too," Phoebe remembered. She smartly saved all the messages on her phone. Her parents showed them to her school and explained what had been going on. The school was able to stop the bullying.

PHONE BULLYING: DO'S AND DON'TS

If you are receiving nasty text messages or calls, there are steps you can take to protect yourself. Here are some ideas for what to do (and what not to do) if you are being bullied by phone:

- Do be careful about giving out your phone number.
- Do save the message. You may need it in order to prove that the bullying has happened.
- Do talk to someone. Receiving a message on your phone is very personal, and bullies will try to make you feel that you are all alone. Explain what is happening to an adult.
- Do stay calm and put the phone down if you receive nasty phone calls.
- Do contact your phone company if you are receiving lots of nasty messages. Even if the number is hidden, the **Internet Service Provider (ISP)** has ways of tracking it down.
- Don't speak first if a call is from a number you do not recognize.
- Don't ever reply to a threatening text. Bullies will often send texts to lots of people to see who replies, and your reply will show that you have been upset by the text.

Email harassment

Bullying by email can happen in lots of different ways. Sometimes a victim will receive one or many insulting or threatening emails. Although this is upsetting, it can be relatively easy to deal with. Most email programs and Internet-based email services like Hotmail or Gmail enable you to block senders if you do not want to receive mail from them (see pages 42 and 43).

But some forms of email bullying can be more difficult to stop. People who want to bully others can easily set up numerous email accounts online. It is difficult to trace the owner of these accounts. Sometimes cyber bullies will set up an account with a name that sounds very similar to their victim's name and send emails pretending to be that person. Often the victim may not know about this.

Protecting yourself

You should never tell anyone the log-in details for your email account. If someone manages to get into your account, it is very difficult to prove that you did not send the emails yourself.

As with bullying text messages, if you receive bullying emails, it is a good idea to keep them. If the bullying continues, you may need to show them to someone as evidence.

If you cannot block the bullies, it is relatively easy to change your own email account (see pages 42 and 43).

COUNT TO TEN

If you are upset or angry about an email or message, do not fire off a reply right away. Find something else to do to take your mind off of being angry, or type a response and read it again later before sending it. People often regret messages they sent when they were angry, so you might end up sending a hurtful message without meaning to.

■ Make sure you only give out personal details, like your email address, to people you trust.

Private emails

Be very careful what you send by email. There are plenty of examples of people who send an email or a private picture to someone, only to find that it has been forwarded to many other people.

You should also be careful about forwarding photos or private messages from friends. This may not be intended to hurt someone, but it could lead to cyber bullying. Remember that photos can always be altered to make them look rude and insulting.

Instant messaging (IM)

Cyber bullies use IM in many ways that are similar to email. You do not always know what person you are actually talking to when you use IM, and people say things using IM that they would not say face-to-face. Private photos and videos can also be sent by IM.

It is easy to be less careful about privacy and security when using IM. You should always understand and check the **privacy settings** on your IM **application** and block anyone who sends bullying messages or who is not on your buddy list.

Chat rooms

Chat rooms are a great way to talk with people online, but they can also be dangerous if you are not careful. Many people who use chat rooms may use different identities. Some chat rooms actually encourage people to use a different identity or **avatar** (character or symbol). Bullying in chat rooms is much more difficult to track than emails and text messages, since the messages from chat rooms cannot be easily saved.

The bullying that happens in chat rooms is often similar to what can happen when any group of people meet together—for example, in a school or club. People in chat rooms can get carried away in a "herd" behavior, and gang up on a single person, making negative comments about what that person says. Groups can also get together with the goal of ignoring certain people within the chat room, which is another form of cyber bullying if it is done on purpose.

The cast of the hit television show *Glee* say they have had lots of friendship requests online from people who once bullied them at school. They have enjoyed fighting back against the bullies by refusing these requests!

Social networking

The growth of social networking sites like Facebook and MySpace in the last few years has been amazing. Facebook has more than 500 million users worldwide. Most young people see these sites as part of their daily lives.

Yet wherever young people meet, either in the real world or online, there will be opportunities for bullying. Cyber bullying can happen through messages posted on personal pages (see the Case Study below) or by pages being created specifically to bully people.

You should be careful about what you post on social networking sites. It is easy to forget how many people can see what you post. Once something is on the site, it is difficult to remove completely. It is best to think before saying anything or uploading photos that might hurt others, or that you might regret yourself. As with all online accounts, never give your password to anyone else.

CASE STUDY

Caught on Facebook

In July 2009, Keeley Houghton was jailed for three months for posting threatening messages on Facebook. Houghton had been bullying a fellow teenager for many years. She had a history of bullying and claimed that she had posted the threats late at night and removed them soon afterward. However, the court found that the threats had been on Facebook for around 24 hours.

Bullying on websites

Social networking sites are not the only websites used for cyber bullying. Websites can be very public, as they can be accessed by anyone connected to the Internet. For example, 15-year-old Jodi Plumb was horrified when she discovered that a website had been set up to bully her. She found out about it when a classmate took a photo of her to include on the website.

Personal polling sites are also used in cyber bullying. These kinds of polls can be hurtful, such as voting for the ugliest kid in a class.

Gaming

Online gaming is growing in popularity all the time, particularly with the constant growth of **MMORPGs** (Massive Multiplayer Online Role-Playing Games) like *World of Warcraft*. These games include chat rooms and discussion **forums**.

As with any game, players often get frustrated with each other in the heat of the game. People will often be very aggressive and rude in what they say and do online. This kind of aggressive interaction is called "**flaming**."

ANONYMOUS—OR NOT?

In 2010 the company that owns the popular MMORPG game *World of Warcraft* recognized that if players did not use their real names, they were much more likely to say and do things online that they would not do if people knew their real identities. (See the box on page 18 for more on this topic.)

The company, called Blizzard, tried to introduce a rule that people taking part in its forums had to use their real name when posting. But the game's players were outraged. They would lose their privacy and open themselves up to being contacted by people from around the world. The company gave in. Although people are more likely to cyber bully if they are not using their own names, it was decided that losing players' privacy would be even worse.

■ *World of Warcraft* is one of the most popular MMORPGs. Just as with any other website, make sure you do not give out any personal information when you play any games online.

GRIEFERS

"Griefers" are bullies who try to make life unpleasant for those playing games online. If you have ever played online games, you have probably come across griefers at one time or another. They may make trouble by harassing beginners, using bad language, or not working as part of a team. Other techniques they use include disrupting the game itself, for example by blocking paths or luring monsters toward other players. Here are some tips for dealing with griefers:

- Don't react to the griefers. If you ignore them, they may get bored. Don't try to beat them by using their tactics and disrupting the game.
- Try to find games that have strict rules to limit griefers. You can also change settings and play private games to limit griefers.
- Never give out personal information, no matter how much you are **provoked** by the griefers.

Cyberstalking

If someone is consistently tracked and harassed using email, IM, social networking sites, or any other electronic media, then that is known as **cyberstalking**. According to Dr. Parry Aftab, a lawyer who specializes in cyber bullying, cyberstalkers fall into three groups:

Failed relationships

Cyberstalking is often the result of a failed relationship. For example, an ex-boyfriend may bombard his ex-girlfriend with emails and text messages. In a survey, 1 in 3 teenagers said that they have been obsessively emailed or texted by a boyfriend or girlfriend checking up on them. Bitter ex-boyfriends and ex-girlfriends may pass private messages and photos on to others or post them on the Internet.

DISINHIBITION

Why do so many people act inappropriately on the Internet? When people communicate online, it is not usually possible to see or hear reactions to what other people say or do. People can also use different usernames and passwords to disguise their true identities. This distance between people and their audience can cause people to do or say things that they might not say if they were talking face-to-face with someone. This is called "**disinhibition**," and it may lead people to say hurtful things online.

"An ex-boyfriend ... started emailing me and saying that he was gonna come to my house and kill me... So, it was getting kind of scary. Yeah, he would say stuff to my friends online too, so I kind of freaked out."

Teenage victim of cyberstalking, quoted in Robin M. Kowalski, Susan P. Limber, and Patricia W. Agatston, *Cyber Bullying: Bullying in the Digital Age* (Malden, MA: Blackwell, 2008.)

Terminated online relationships

When an online relationship ends, the stalker and his or her victim have not met in real life. They have formed a relationship in a chat room or similar online meeting place, and the relationship has fallen apart, possibly because of the obsessive behavior that becomes cyberstalking. The victim will have shared some private information, but the stalker will also gather information about the victim from across the Internet.

Random cyberstalkers

Random cyberstalkers like the idea of scaring people online. They may meet people online with the intention of stalking them.

Tracking down the victim

Cyberstalkers are scarier than most types of cyber bullies because they can move from online harassment to stalking someone in the real world. They will find as much as they can about the person on the Internet. Even if you are careful about what information you post online, it can be relatively easy for someone to find things like your street address and phone number—if someone knows your real name. In extreme cases, it can be possible to track things like your cell phone to find out where you are.

■ It is tough when a relationship ends. In rare cases, this can lead to cyberstalking.

"Happy slapping"

The phrase "**happy slapping**" makes this type of cyber bullying sound like fun. Unfortunately, it is not at all fun for those on the receiving end of it. In a happy slapping attack, one person physically attacks someone, while another person records the attack, often with a cell phone camera. The video of the incident is then posted online or sent from phone to phone for others to watch. This type of bullying is designed to threaten and **humiliate** the victim, who may be someone unknown to his or her attackers.

Happy slapping attacks often involve more than a slap and can be very serious. Triston Christmas was 18 years old when he was attacked during a night out. Triston was punched to the ground and later died after hitting his head on a concrete floor. His attackers continued to film as Triston lay on the ground with blood coming from his mouth and ear. They then went to a party and sent the film of the attack to their friends. Triston's attackers were arrested and taken to court for this and several other attacks.

Happy slapping and the law

Happy slapping stories show that cyber bullying can cause physical harm, just like other forms of bullying. Any physical attack is always against the law. (For more on cyber bullying and the law, see pages 46 and 47.) By filming their crimes, happy slappers give police and the courts all the evidence they need to convict the attackers of a serious crime.

"Being hit in public, which is what historically bullying has been about, is ... humiliating enough, but in general it was limited to just the small number of people who would be standing around at the time it happened... What's far, far worse is the way that [happy slapping attack victims'] humiliation is being multiplied and advertised and broadcast to people they [the victim] know and people they don't know."

John Carr, adviser on Internet safety, quoted on the ABC News program *Nightline*, 2006

■ Has someone ever sent you bullying pictures and videos? If you send them on to other people, you are joining in with the bullying.

OTHER ONLINE DANGERS

This book is about cyber bullying, which, as we have seen, normally happens between young people in a variety of ways. But many of the tricks used by cyber bullies, such as using false identities or setting up multiple email addresses, may also be used by adults who are trying to harm young people. The Internet brings many benefits, but there is always a minority of dangerous people who misuse it. You should always be careful about giving out any personal details, and talk to a trusted adult if you are concerned about anything that has happened online.

WHO ARE CYBER BULLIES?

What makes a person a cyber bully? Often the cyber bully has the same qualities as a traditional bully.

Types of traditional bullies

Research has found many different types of traditional bully. Do you recognize any of these types?

- Social bullies are people who pretend to be nice, but who use sneaky tactics to bully people. Social bullies spread rumors and tease people, often behind their victims' backs.
- Confident bullies are people who feel good when wielding power over others. Confident bullies often want people to see them in action.
- Fully armored bullies are cold and **calculating**. They know exactly what they are doing. They can be charming, but this is usually not sincere. They plan carefully and like to stay hidden.

WHAT ARE BULLIES LIKE?

Research has shown that most bullies share several characteristics, whether they choose to bully people on the playground or with electronic media:

- They have a strong need to dominate other people and get their own way.
- They show little sympathy for the feelings of their victims.
- They are defiant and aggressive toward adults and not good at following rules.
- They act on impulse and lose their temper easily.

- Many bullies are people who have been bullied themselves.
- Some people would not be bullies on their own, but when they get together, they bully others. They know it is wrong, but they do it to impress their friends. Doing something because other people are doing it is called peer pressure.
- A gang of bullies is well-organized and deliberately sets out to cause harm. They use violence to control their turf.

The same as cyber bullies?

All of these types of traditional bully may also get involved in cyber bullying. However, some cyber bullies are often different from the traditional bully.

One common type of bully is called the confident bully. Confident bullies usually want to make sure other people see them in action, because they feel good having power over others.

Bullying in secret

Many people who become cyber bullies are not the sort of people who would take part in traditional bullying. These people are sometimes comfortable with cyber bullying because they believe they are less likely to get caught. They like the fact that the victim does not know who is bullying them.

Reasons for cyber bullying

There are several different types of cyber bully, according to the group stopcyberbullying.org:

The power-hungry cyber bully

Power-hungry cyber bullies are the closest to the traditional playground bully. They often want people to see them as powerful, so they are less likely to hide their identities. Sometimes they may not be physically strong enough to be a physical bully, so they try to wield power online.

The "vengeful angel"

"Vengeful angels" use online bullying to get back at people. In many cases, they may have been bullied themselves, and so they might think that cyber bullying is their only way to fight back.

It can be difficult to stand up against a group who are bullying others, but it is the right thing to do.

The bored bully

Some cyber bullies act out of boredom. They are more interested in amusing themselves than in really hurting their victim. These cyber bullies might act in a group and encourage each other to bully.

The accidental cyber bully

There are also people who cyber bully others without realizing it. This could be because they have been tricked into bullying someone—for example, by replying to an email sent by the bully while pretending to be the victim. It could also be because they accidentally said something to hurt someone's feelings or made someone feel left out.

THE HIDDEN CYBER BULLY

Sometimes cyber bullies will get someone else to do the bullying for them. This is called cyber bullying by proxy. Often the people who do the bullying do not know they are doing it. Here are a few examples of how this can work:

- The cyber bully pretends to be the intended victim—either by accessing that person's account or by setting up an account with a very similar name. The bully then sends nasty messages or posts rude comments about the victim's friends. These friends think their friend has turned on them. They start to lash out against their former friend.

- Some cyber bullies will get their victim barred from a website. While chatting online, they will provoke the victim into sending a reply that breaks the rules of the site. When the victim sends the reply, the bully then uses the "warning" button. The moderator of the site may then ban the victim, without realizing that the person was provoked by someone else. Someone who deliberately provokes others online is called a **troll**.

- One of the most dangerous types of bullying is to post someone's personal details online. This might be on an established public website or on a specially created site. These details can then get into the hands of some very dangerous people.

Are you a cyber bully?

After reading about the different kinds of cyber bullies, is it possible you are a cyber bully yourself? If so, how can you stop?

If you are bullying alone, you can make the choice to stop doing it right away. But for many people, cyber bullying is not a conscious choice they make. A group of friends may have gotten you involved in it and, once you are involved, it can be very difficult to say, "Stop! I'm not doing this anymore." Many people admit to forwarding emails or joining in bullying simply because their friends are doing it.

You should think about the effect of what you and your friends are doing. You may not see the victim, but can you imagine how he or she is feeling? How would you feel if you were in that position? You should also make the effort to apologize to your victim.

CASE STUDY

I was a cyber bully

A group of teenagers in the library was asked what they did online that their parents would not approve of. A shy, intelligent boy put his hand up. He said he sent death threats by email.

He was the kind of boy who always did well in school and would never dream of hurting anyone in real life, so why did he send these emails? "Because I can" was his answer. This good student pretended to be someone else online and did not think he could get caught. He also could not see the hurt and distress that his actions caused to his victims. (This story is taken from the www.stopcyberbullying.org website, set up by Parry Aftab.)

HOW MANY PEOPLE HAVE CYBER BULLIED OTHERS?

Most research has revealed that 1 in 3 teenagers say they have taken part in some kind of cyber bullying, although some reports put the figure lower than that. The most common ways that people admitted to cyber bullying others were by posting nasty comments online or by forwarding emails that spread rumors about people. Think about what you do online and messages you have sent. Have you ever cyber bullied anyone, either on purpose or by accident?

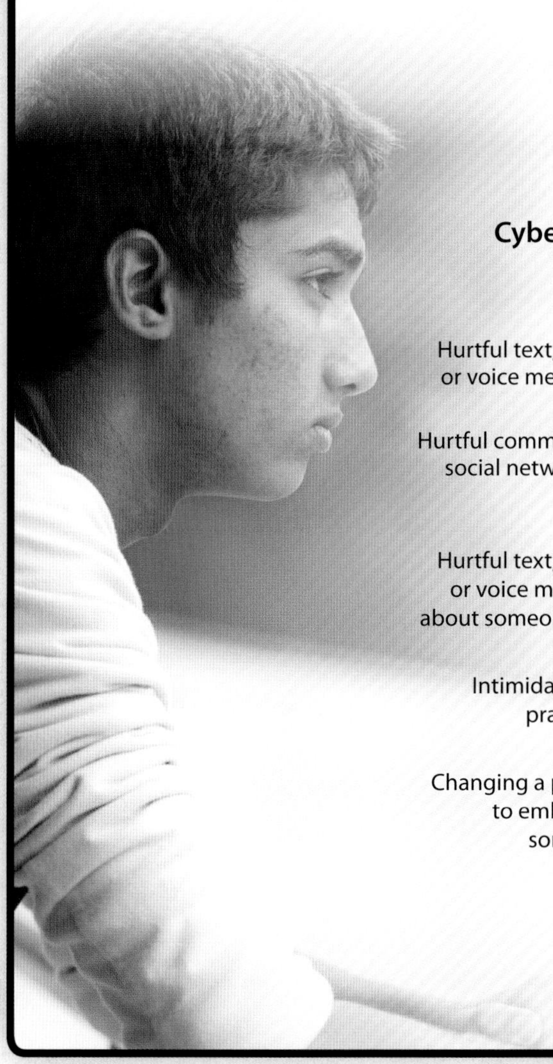

This chart shows the different types of cyber bullying that young people have admitted to.

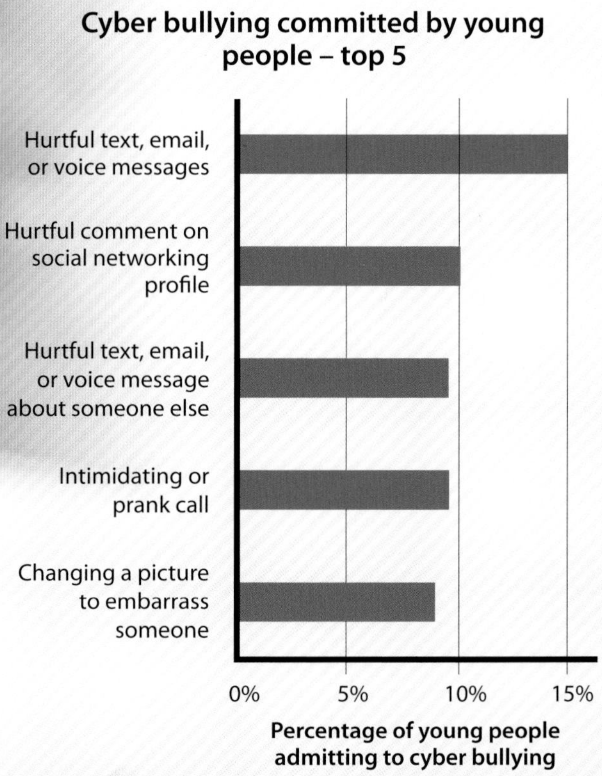
Cyber bullying committed by young people – top 5
Hurtful text, email, or voice messages
Hurtful comment on social networking profile
Hurtful text, email, or voice message about someone else
Intimidating or prank call
Changing a picture to embarrass someone
0%
5%
10%
15%
Percentage of young people admitting to cyber bullying

What if my friend is a cyber bully?

Even if you have never cyber bullied people, it is quite likely that you know cyber bullies. If you are worried that friends are cyber bullying someone else, talk to them about it. It may be easier if a group of friends can talk to the person doing the bullying.

You do not need to accuse friends of being bullies. They might not even know they are doing it if it is just a misunderstanding that made someone feel left out (see box below). Otherwise, what seems like fun or a "prank" to those who are doing it may be much nastier to the person on the receiving end.

If your friends do realize they are cyber bullying, they may give a number of reasons to justify what they are doing. It is easy to say that everyone else is doing it, or that the victim deserves it for some reason. If this is the case, try to make them think about what they are doing from the point of view of the victim. Because it does not happen face-to-face, cyber bullies often do not see the pain it causes their victims (see the box on page 18).

Discover the facts

If the cyber bullying continues, find out more about why your friends are doing it. Your friends may be acting out because they have been bullied themselves.

If you are concerned that the cyber bullying will not stop, you should think about telling an adult. This is a difficult decision to make, as it will likely affect your friendship if the cyber bully finds out. However, as the stories in this book show, cyber bullying can have serious consequences for the victims—and for the people doing the cyber bullying.

FEELING LEFT OUT

It is important for people to feel included or part of the "in" crowd. Has a friend ever made you feel left out because he or she did not send a quick reply to an IM or text message? If people do not receive a reply to comments or messages, they sometimes feel like they are being deliberately excluded from a group of friends. If this is being done on purpose, it could be cyber bullying. But it also could just be that people forget to reply or do not realize that not replying is hurting someone's feelings.

If you cannot get friends to stop cyber bullying, make it clear that you do not agree with what they are doing and consider talking to an adult.

WITNESSES TO CYBER BULLYING

Many young people have seen cyber bullying in action, perhaps as they watch their friends. Most commonly this is through seeing a comment in an IM session or on a social networking site like Facebook or MySpace. Many young people have watched bullying on sites like YouTube, where bullying videos designed to embarrass victims are often posted.

WHO IS AFFECTED BY CYBER BULLYING?

Cyber bullying can affect anyone. We have already seen that some cyber bullying, like happy slapping attacks, can be random. When cyber bullying happens in chat rooms and online games, the people doing the bullying do not know their victim. But many cyber bullies know their victims.

Likely targets

Many people who are affected by traditional bullying are also victims of cyber bullying. All bullies will often pick on the people they see as weak, vulnerable, or having low **self-esteem**. A bully might prey on something that a victim is self-conscious about, such as the way he or she looks.

Traditionally, bullies may also pick on those who look different or stand out from the crowd in some way. This kind of bullying could include **racism** or attacks against people who are thought to be gay.

Traditional bullies may pick on someone who looks different or is less able to deal with physical threats. Cyber bullies may pick on anyone.

Teachers as targets

Many people believe that cyber bullying only happens between young people. However, teachers have also been targets for cyber bullies, with a quarter of all teachers saying they were aware of websites that had been set up to embarrass and bully teachers. Students have created fake websites or social networking profiles for teachers or principals, often spreading vicious or untrue rumors. Schools take this kind of bullying very seriously, and it can lead to being expelled from school or even legal action.

Yet cyber bullies can pick on other targets, too. Because the bullies' identities can be hidden, they might choose targets they would not be bold enough to attack face-to-face. These people could be popular at school and not the usual targets for other bullies. They can even be adults such as teachers.

CASE STUDY

Alex

Alex was a "vibrant and sporty" girl from a small town in New Zealand. Alex had been cyber bullied for months. A group of older girls sent her emails and text messages threatening her and telling her not to come to school. Alex showed the messages to her mother, who told the school. Even though the school contacted the bullies' parents, the abuse continued. Alex took her own life the day before school started in 2006, at the age of 12.

"Maybe people need to understand you don't actually have to do anything wrong to be bullied."

Deanne Teka, mother of Alex, who took her own life in 2006

Boys and girls

Before cyber bullying came along, bullying tended to affect boys more than girls, because of the emphasis on physical threats and violence. With cyber bullying, the picture is very different. Girls are more likely to be cyber bullied than boys.

In a survey of a large school district in the United States, 25 percent of girls said they had been cyber bullied, compared to 16 percent of boys. In the same survey, more girls also admitted to cyber bullying others—although some other surveys have found that there are a roughly equal proportion of boys and girls who cyber bully others.

Girls and boys favor different types of cyber bullying. Boys are more likely to make prank phone calls and to record acts of bullying. Girls are more likely to send texts and hurtful messages. Girls are also much more likely to send messages about the victim to other people.

Why is being cyber bullied so painful?

If people are unable to stop being cyber bullied, it can affect them very badly—even to the point of taking their own lives (see box at right). Why is the experience of being cyber bullied so painful for these people?

■ More girls than boys are affected by cyber bullying. Girls are also more likely to use social networking sites, with 4 in 10 girls saying that these sites are an important part of their lives.

CYBER BULLYING AND SUICIDE

Cyber bullying can have terrible effects on those who experience it. There are many examples—like the example of Alex on page 31 and the example of Megan Meier on pages 34 and 35—of young people who have felt so trapped by cyber bullying that they have been driven to take their own lives. Recent research has revealed that teenagers who have experienced cyber bullying are more than twice as likely to have attempted suicide than those who have not been cyber bullied.

One of the worst things about cyber bullying is that there can seem to be no escape. We live in an "always on" society. We always have our cell phones with us or our computers nearby. This means that cyber bullies can always get to us. Even if someone turns off a phone or computer, the messages are still there. If cyber bullies use websites, the victim knows that the bullying is always there for others to see.

Also, one of a cyber bully's biggest weapons is that a victim does not always know who his or her bully is. As a result, the person being targeted can start to lose trust in everyone.

■ Finding opportunities to get away from electronic media can seem harder than ever for some young people. But it is a good idea to take a break, especially to spend time with friends.

CASE STUDY

Megan Meier

Megan Meier was just like most 13 year olds in Dardenne Prairie, Missouri. She was interested in swimming, dogs, hip-hop music, and boys. Megan had her problems. For one thing, she was self-conscious about being overweight. Megan had also suffered from depression and was seeing a therapist.

In November 2006 things were looking good for Megan. She was at a new school, had lost weight, and was on the volleyball team. On top of that, a boy named Josh Evans had contacted her through the social networking site MySpace. Josh said he had just moved to the area from Florida. He was not going to regular school and did not yet have a phone number at his new house.

Suddenly, things changed. On October 15, 2006, Josh sent Megan a message saying: "I don't know if I want to be friends with you anymore because I've heard that you are not very nice to your friends."

Megan was shocked. She did not know who Josh had been talking to. The next day she logged on again, only to find more nasty messages from Josh. Her mother, Tina, was just going out and told her daughter to leave the website and ignore the messages. Megan said she would, but she became more and more distressed as she received hurtful and insulting messages from different people. It seemed like Josh had shared some of their private messages.

When Tina returned home, she found her daughter sending angry replies to some of the messages. Tina and Megan argued, after which Megan went to her room. Twenty minutes later, Tina went to check on her daughter and found that Megan had hanged herself. Megan died the next day.

The truth about "Josh"

Megan's parents tried to contact Josh Evans to tell him the effect his messages had had on their daughter. They found that his MySpace account had been closed.

They later discovered that "Josh" did not exist at all. The mother of one of Megan's friends, helped by someone who worked for her, had pretended to be "Josh" on MySpace. The woman said that she had been trying to find out what Megan was saying about her own daughter. At the time, cyber bullying

Megan Meier's mother said that Megan was "the happiest she had ever been" before her cyber bullying nightmare began.

was not illegal, and so no one was convicted of a crime in connection with Megan's death.

Megan's story shows the harm that cyber bullying has done to one family. It also shows that people may not always spot the signs of a fake identity if they want to believe that someone is who they say they are.

MEGAN MEIER FOUNDATION

Megan's parents set up a foundation to make people more aware of the harm that cyber bullying can do. Megan's mother travels around the United States speaking to young people about the dangers. She has also worked with lawmakers in Missouri to make cyber bullying illegal.

DEALING WITH THE PAIN CAUSED BY CYBER BULLYING

Clearly, cyber bullying can cause a lot of pain. If you are being affected by cyber bullying, this book contains lots of practical advice on how to stop it. But how can you deal with the pain caused by cyber bullying?

Talking it through

Remember that cyber bullying is not your fault, and that there are lots of people who will listen. You should start by talking to trusted friends and adults, either at home or at school. The people who know you best should be able to give you the best advice. Some young people are reluctant to talk to adults, but with some cyber bullying this is necessary and the only way to stop it.

If you are being cyber bullied, you may be reluctant to talk about it. But talking will help you to feel less isolated.

Other sources of help

There are lots of websites and organizations that can provide advice and ideas on how to deal with cyber bullying (see pages 54 and 55). Many of these websites will include stories of people who have overcome cyber bullying.

Websites that you use, such as social networking sites, should also contain advice on privacy and safety online. They may also include advice on cyber bullying.

It is important not to suffer in silence. No matter how difficult things may seem, there is always a way out of cyber bullying, as well as someone who can help. You are unlikely to be the only person you know who is affected.

CASE STUDY

Fighting back

Steve had been bullied for many years. Taunts about his weight and physical attacks had been followed by cyber bullying through his page on the social networking website Bebo. At the age of 13, Steve considered taking his own life. "The bullies made me feel worthless," he said. "I felt uncomfortable and unhappy within myself and I didn't want to be alive anymore."

After reaching his lowest point, Steve talked to friends and teachers about his ordeal. This helped, and he decided to fight back by concentrating on his schoolwork. Steve became a leader at his school and used his experience of being bullied to set up an anti–bullying program at school, encouraging people to talk about their experiences with bullying.

Helping a friend who is being bullied

It can be difficult to watch friends be hurt by cyber bullies. But how can you help them? People often keep cyber bullying to themselves. Maybe they are embarrassed or feel they have done something wrong to cause the bullying. Also, if they do not know who is doing the bullying, they may be unsure about whom they can trust to talk to about it. Hopefully they will trust you enough to tell you about it.

■ Young people who live in your neighborhood and appear quite normal might be suffering through cyber bullying in silence.

Being there for them

Remember that people being bullied may be very emotional, so they may not be thinking clearly about the best things to do, such as blocking the phone numbers or email addresses of the bullies. You can help your friends think of basic solutions like this. You should not get involved with the bullies directly, however. This may create further problems or involve you in the bullying. The best thing you can do is be a good friend.

LOOKING FOR SIGNS

There are some signs you can look for if you suspect your friends may be victims of cyber bullying. Some of the most common signs are:

- They start staying home from school when they have not done so in the past.
- They change how they use the Internet, either by using it much more than previously or appearing to lose interest altogether.
- They become secretive about their Internet use—for example, by not sharing things that they would have shared previously or minimizing windows when anyone approaches them.
- They do not answer their phone or check texts constantly when they are with other people.
- They become **antisocial** and do not join in with friends.
- They are out sick a lot and fall behind with schoolwork.

Any major change in your friends' behavior could be a sign of cyber bullying. You can also ask other friends if they have noticed anything or if they know of any cyber bullying. (Be aware, however, that these signs could reflect other issues in a young person's life as well.)

If someone suddenly stops joining in with friends or changes his or her behavior, it could be a sign that that person is being cyber bullied.

Raising awareness

You can also help yourself and your friends by raising awareness about cyber bullying. If cyber bullying is a problem at your school, encourage the school to organize events to help people understand what cyber bullying is. Your fellow students can find out how to get help if they are being bullied. They may also be forced to look more closely at the issue if they have been bullying others. You could organize an anti-bullying week.

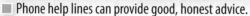 Phone help lines can provide good, honest advice.

ANTI-BULLYING AWARENESS

On April 20, 1999, two students at Columbine High School, near Littleton, Colorado, killed 12 other students, a teacher, and took their own lives in one of the United States' worst school shootings. Both students saw their killing spree as revenge for the bullying they had suffered. In memory of the tragedy, the third week of April is now a week for raising awareness of bullying in the United States. Anti-bullying organizations and schools organize events to raise awareness of bullying and how to deal with it.

Schools can do a lot to make people more aware of cyber bullying. They can also provide mentors who understand how young people use technology. These people can provide help with solving problems. If you do not feel comfortable talking to anyone you know, there are lots of other places you can go for help and advice.

Mentors

Anti-bullying organizations such as Teenangels (see page 55) have trained teenagers so that young people will have someone their own age to talk to about cyber bullying.

For example, Jane discovered nasty comments appearing on her MySpace page, making fun of her weight and how she looked. She talked to Kathy, an online mentor. Kathy was able to trace who had sent the messages. She also discovered that the girl responsible had been bullying other people. Kathy reported the issue to the school, and adults were able to stop the bullying.

HOW TO STOP CYBER BULLYING

As we have discussed, there are many actions you can take to protect yourself from cyber bullies. To review, these action include:

- Guard your privacy carefully. This will make it more difficult for cyber bullies to reach you. You should only share your contact details with people you trust. You can have an email address or online identity that only your family and closest friends know about.
- You should also be careful about how much information you post about yourself online, such as details of where you live, or photos.
- Never respond to an abusive message.
- Be very careful when you receive any emails from people you don't know. If in doubt, don't open them.
- Save any bullying messages, as this can serve as evidence.
- Tell an adult what is going on if the bullying becomes a problem.
- But beyond these basic steps, what else can you do to stop cyber bullies?

PRIVACY SETTINGS

What are the privacy settings on your social-network profiles? Many of the hundreds of millions of people who use social networking sites do not know the answer to this question. It is a good idea to set up your privacy settings so that only friends can view your profile. This is not usually the **default** setting, so you will have to change the settings yourself. Also, be careful when accepting people as friends on these sites. Cyber bullies could set up fake profiles.

Blocking bullies

The best way to beat a cyber bully is to block him or her from getting to you. As we have seen, most email applications will allow you to block senders. You could also send emails straight to a folder so that you do not have to read them. If cyber bullying comes through IM, you can block or ignore the contact.

Blocking may not be a permanent solution, however. It is easy for a cyber bully to set up an account in another name. If blocking senders does not solve your problems, you may have to close your email or IM account and open a new one. This will give you the chance to protect your privacy by only giving your new address to people you trust. If blocking the senders does not stop the bullying, you should talk to an adult.

You can prevent email bullying by only giving your email address to friends and family.

Banning bullies

If you are having problems with bullies who misuse social networking sites and chat rooms, you can report them. Social networking and online gaming sites should be able to ban cyber bullies.

Removing websites

If cyber bullying takes place on a public website, it is more difficult to ignore, and it cannot be blocked. You have control over your own profile on social networking sites, so you can block other users from posting comments. If a fake profile has been set up, however, you will need to contact the owner of the website to get it taken down. If there is no obvious way to do this, there should be details of how to contact customer service on the site. YouTube also allows you to report offensive videos and get them taken down.

Although most websites have a policy of removing bullying content, some people have complained that websites do not always respond immediately. This can be distressing for someone who is being cyber bullied and just wants the bullying to go away. If you are dealing with an offensive website, talk to an adult about it. If you are not able to get it taken down immediately, contact the police.

TRACING CYBER BULLIES

If you receive bullying messages by phone, you can contact the phone company. They can track the person who owns the number.

Social networking sites and other websites can track the **IP address** of the computer that was used to post bullying material. They may only do this if requested by the police. No matter how much people think they can remain hidden on the Internet, they always leave a trail that can be tracked by police and ISPs.

BANNING SOCIAL NETWORKING SITES?

A middle school principal in New Jersey sent a letter to parents asking them to ban their teenagers from using social networking sites. He wrote, "There is absolutely no reason for any middle school student to be a part of a social networking site!" You might think this is a bit extreme, but people do need to take precautions to reduce the risk of cyber bullying.

Parents are usually very understanding about issues like cyber bullying.

Cyber bullying and the law

If cyber bullying cannot be stopped, school officials or even the police could get involved. Cyber bullying is not a crime in itself in most places, although as people find out more about it, there are calls for it to be made a crime. Yet cyber bullying can involve criminal behavior, which the police will take seriously. For example:

- Any kind of physical attack, such as a happy slapping attack, is a crime, especially if it causes physical harm.
- Threats being made against a particular person are a crime.
- Cyberstalking or harassment may be crimes, depending on the number of messages or threats a victim receives.
- Spreading false rumors online that could affect someone's reputation, whether that person is another teenager or an adult such as a teacher, can sometimes be a crime.

CYBER BULLIES IN COURT

One of the most extreme examples of a cyber bullying crime was committed by a group of older teenage boys in a suburb of Melbourne, Australia. The gang filmed a number of serious "happy slapping" attacks that they distributed online and on DVD. The gang was exposed by a television investigation after gang members sold copies of the film at local schools. These less-than-smart bullies were so sure they would not be caught that they included their real names in the credits. Eleven young people were charged with serious crimes, and most were placed on supervision orders, meaning that they had to report regularly and do work for the community.

Consequences

Even if the cyber bullying does not end up in court, it can still be serious for those involved. In terms of use of the Internet, it may result in cyber bullies being banned by ISPs and social networking sites. The history of what you do online can follow you around for a long time, and it can be very difficult to take something back once it is on the Internet.

In terms of bullies' personal lives, cyber bullying can lead to students being suspended—or even expelled—from school. This will have a hugely negative impact on future attempts to get into college and even to get future jobs. Mistakes people make when they are young can stick with them for life.

Cyber bullying can have a big impact on the education of both those who do the bullying and their victims. Schools usually treat it very seriously.

DEBATING CYBER BULLYING

This book has looked at the many ways that cyber bullying can affect young people's lives, and how to deal with it. There is no debate about whether cyber bullying is a bad thing. But it does raise some questions about how technology affects our lives. Can we find a balance between sharing our lives online with old and new friends, while not opening ourselves up to becoming targets for cyber bullying?

Here are some debates raised by the contents of this book, including arguments for and against. Consider the issues and decide what you think about these debates. Can you think of other arguments?

Young people should be banned from social networking sites

Arguments for:

- The amount of cyber bullying that happens on these sites and the other dangers posed by social networking show that they are bad for young people's health. Other health dangers are restricted for teenagers, so why not social networking?
- The big corporations that run social networking sites have not done enough to protect young people, so the law needs to be changed to protect them.
- Some young people do not have the maturity to behave properly online, so they should be banned for their own safety.

Arguments against:

- Victims of bullying, and young people in general, should not be punished for the actions of cyber bullies and adults.
- Age limits are easy to get around, since people can pretend to be someone else online. Also, there are already age limits on many social networking sites.
- Young people need to learn how to behave on the Internet by using these sites.
- If you ban young people from social networking sites, people will just find another way to cyber bully.

Cyber bullying is not as bad as physical bullying

Arguments for:

- Cyber bullying does not usually do any physical harm to the victim.
- Some cyber bullying can be ignored or avoided by blocking senders and making sure you protect your privacy online.
- No one forces you to go online or to use IM. Physical bullies harass people in the real world.

Arguments against:

- Cyber bullying can be more mentally damaging than other types of bullying. Many victims have harmed themselves as a result.
- The freedom to do things online or to use a cell phone without being cyber bullied is just as important as being able to go to school without being bullied.
- Cyber bullying can affect people 24 hours a day, so it is much more difficult to escape.

Stand up against cyber bullying

No matter what you think about these debates, cyber bullying is certainly a serious issue. Teenagers will continue to use the Internet and cell phones, and new types of cyber bullying will continue to develop. Although society is becoming more aware of the dangers, the only people who can really prevent cyber bullying are young people themselves—by making it clear that it is never acceptable to bully someone else using electronic media.

■ Physical bullying can be very nasty, but is it really worse than cyber bullying?

49

CYBER BULLYING QUICK TIPS

Technology	Type of cyber bullying	Prevention and solutions
Cell phone	• threatening text messages and calls • taking and circulating nasty photos • happy slapping attacks	• Protect your phone with a password or **Personal Identification Number (PIN)**. • Only give your number to trusted people. • Block callers or senders of messages and save harassing messages. • Don't reply to or pass on bullying texts. • Change your phone number if the bullying does not stop.
Instant messaging (IM)	• threatening and nasty messages • using someone else's account to send messages that will embarrass that person	• Never share your password. • Be careful of which people you include on your list of friends. • Ban or ignore people who send threatening messages. • Don't respond to bullying messages. • Don't give out personal information.
Chat rooms and message boards	• flaming • groups ganging up or ignoring someone • trolling • people pretending to be someone they're not	• Don't give out personal information. • Don't respond to bullying messages. • Don't join in with bullying others. • Be wary of people you don't know personally.
Email	• threatening and nasty emails • false rumors sent to a large group of people • using someone's account to pretend to be that person	• Never share your password. • Don't respond to bullying emails. • Block senders of threatening emails and save the messages. • Don't open an email if you don't know the sender. • Don't forward bullying emails to other people.

Technology	Type of cyber bullying	Prevention and solutions
Social networking sites	• threatening and nasty messages • posting embarrassing photos and videos • ganging up on people • people pretending to be someone they're not or setting up fake profiles	• Never share your password. • Set privacy settings so only friends can see your profile. • Be careful of which people you include on your list of friends. • Don't give out personal information. • Report misuse to the website.
Video-sharing sites and other websites	• posting embarrassing or threatening content for all to see, including happy slapping videos • people pretending to be someone they're not	• Report misuse to the website or ISP. • Report abusive or fake websites to the police.
Gaming sites	• griefers • abusive remarks • flaming • picking on less experienced users and killing their characters	• Report misuse to the website. • Don't give out your personal information. • Don't respond to bullying messages. • Don't join in with bullying of others. • Be wary of people you don't know personally.

INTERNET SLANG

The following are a few terms of Internet slang that you may or may not know:

Slang	Meaning
A/S/L	age/sex/location (but never give these details to someone you don't know!)
EOD	end of day or end of discussion
flame war	online discussion that becomes a series of personal attacks
LSHMBH	laughing so hard my belly hurts
newbie	(or "noob"), someone who is new to the Internet or to gaming
ohnosecond	the time it takes you to realize you shouldn't have sent that message
POS	parents over shoulder (also P911 for "parent alert")
XME	excuse me
YGBK	you've gotta be kidding
zerg	to gang up on someone

GLOSSARY

antisocial behavior that harms other people or society in general

application computer program designed to do a particular job, such as an email application that is designed to send emails

avatar character or symbol that people choose to represent them in an online game or chat room

blog short for "weblog," an online journal that is updated regularly

calculating if someone is calculating, they deliberately do things to get a particular reaction, for example a bully calculates how a victim will react

cyberstalking obsessively tracking someone's movements or activity on the Internet. Cyberstalking can lead to stalking in the real world.

default settings that will be used unless the user changes them—for example, the settings that are first installed

disinhibition what happens when we communicate with people via electronic media. We do or say things that we would not if the person was in the same room with us.

electronic media ways of communicating using digital technologies, primarily over the Internet

flaming sending angry or insulting messages on the Internet, such as in a chat room. If people reply to these messages, a "flame war" can develop.

forum online area for discussions where users post topics

happy slapping physical attack that is filmed using a phone or another video camera

harass bully or attack repeatedly

humiliate deliberately make someone feel embarrassed or ashamed

impersonate pretend to be someone else

instant messaging (IM) way of communicating via messages sent in real time, usually to a group of people on a list of friends

Internet Service Provider (ISP) company that provides the means to connect to the Internet. An ISP may also provide other services like email.

IP address series of numbers that is the unique address for any computer connected to the Internet

MMORPG stands for "Massive Multiplayer Online Role-Playing Game," an online game in which thousands of individual gamers compete against each other or work together as teams

persecute pick on someone repeatedly

Personal Identification Number (PIN) unique number people use to identify themselves—for example, when taking money out of an automated teller machine (ATM)

personal polling site website that enables users to set up quick surveys or polls on any topic and invite people to vote

privacy settings settings on a website such as a social networking site that determine what information others can see about a person

provoke to cause a reaction from someone

racism harassing or bullying someone because of where they come from or the color of their skin

self-esteem good opinion of oneself. Low self-esteem means a person does not have a good opinion of himself or herself.

smartphone phone that is also designed for Internet access and running other applications

social networking site website such as Facebook or MySpace that enables users to set up profiles of themselves and interact with friends and other users

troll someone who deliberately makes comments on websites and in chat rooms that are designed to make people angry and to get an aggressive response

FURTHER INFORMATION

Books

Allman, Toney. *Mean Behind the Screen: What You Need to Know about Cyberbullying* (*What's the Issue?* series). Mankato, MN: Compass Point, 2009.

Bingham, Jane. *Taking Action Against Bullying* (*Taking Action* series). New York, NY: Rosen, 2010.

Hile, Lori. *Social Networks and Blogs* (*Mastering Media* series). Chicago, IL: Raintree, 2011.

Jacobs, Thomas A. *Teen Cyberbullying Investigated: Where Do Your Rights End and Consequences Begin?* Minneapolis, MN: Free Spirit, 2010.

Medina, Sarah. *Respect Others, Respect Yourself* (*Life Skills* series). Chicago, IL: Heinemann Library, 2009.

Rooney, Anne. *Bullying* (*Teen FAQ* series). Mankato, MN: Arcturus, 2010.

Websites

www.stopcyberbullying.org

This useful website includes a short presentation and lots of information on cyber bullying, including information about cyber bullying and the law.

www.cyberbullying.org

This Canadian website was created by Bill Belsey, who first used the term "cyber bullying."